Also by Yusef Komunyakaa

THE CHAMELEON COUCH

Farrar, Straus and Giroux New York

THE CHAMELEON COUCH POEMS YUSEF KOMUNYAKAA

THE CHAMELEON COUCH POEMS YUSEF KOMUNYAKAA

THE CHAMELEON COUCH POEMS YUSEF KOMUNYAKAA

THE CHAMELEON COUCH POEMS YUSEF KOMUNYAKAA

THE CHAMELEON COUCH POEMS YUSEF KOMUNYAKAA

THE CHAMELEON COUCH POEMS YUSEF KOMUNYAKAA

THE CHAMELEON COUCH POEMS YUSEF KOMUNYAKAA

THE CHAMELEON COUCH POEMS YUSEF KOMUNYAKAA

Farrar, Straus and Giroux
18 West 18th Street, New York 10011

Copyright © 2011 by Yusef Komunyakaa
All rights reserved
Distributed in Canada by D&M Publishers, Inc.
Printed in the United States of America
First edition, 2011

Grateful acknowledgment is made to the following publications,
in which some of these poems originally appeared: *The American
Poetry Review*, *The Believer*, *Calabash*, *Callaloo*, *Cerise*, *Dossier*,
Dublin Poetry Review, *Five Points*, *Gulf Coast*, *The Harvard Review*,
Indiana Review, *Mantis*, *The New Ohio Review*, *The New Republic*,
New York City Port Authority, *The New Yorker*, *The New York Times*,
The Northwest Review, *Open City*, *Oxford Quarterly*, *Parnassus*,
Ploughshares, *PN Review*, *Poetry*, *Salt*, and *Semicerchio*.

The image on page 66 is from Andrea Mantegna's
"Allegory of Vice and Virtue."

Library of Congress Cataloging-in-Publication Data
Komunyakaa, Yusef.
    The chameleon couch : poems / Yusef Komunyakaa.— 1st ed.
    p. cm.
    ISBN: 978-0-374-12038-2 (alk. paper)
    I. Title.

PS3561.O455C48 2011
811'.54—dc22

                                                    2010033148

Designed and composed by Quemadura

www.fsgbooks.com

10 9 8 7 6 5 4 3 2 1

For Iwona and Jerzy Jakubiak,
thanks for your kindness in Czestochowa

CONTENTS

I

I I

III

CANTICLE

Because I mistrust my head & hands, because I know salt
    tinctures my songs, I tried hard not to touch you
even as I pulled you into my arms. Seasons sprouted
    & went to seed as we circled the dance with silver cat bells
tied to our feet. Now, kissing you, I am the archheir of second
      chances.
    Because I know twelve ways to be wrong
& two to be good, I was wounded by the final question in the cave,
    left side of the spirit level's quiver. I didn't want to hug you
into a cross, but I'm here to be measured down to each numbered
      bone.
    A trembling runs through what pulls us to the blood knot.
We hold hands & laugh in the East Village as midnight autumn
    shakes the smoke of the Chicago B.L.U.E.S. club from our clothes,
& you say I make you happy & sad. For years I stopped my hands
    in midair, knowing fire at the root stem of yes.
I say your name, & another dies in my mouth because I know how
      to plead
    till a breeze erases the devil's footprints,
because I crave something to sing the blues about. Look,
    I only want to hold you this way: a bundle of wild orchids
broken at the wet seam of memory & manna.

THE JANUS PREFACE

The day breaks in half as the sun rolls over hanging ice,
& a dogwood leans into a country between seasons.
A yellow cat looms with feet in the squishy snow,
arching her back, eyeing a redbird, a star still blinking
in her nighttime brain. Schoolgirls sport light dresses
beneath heavy coats, & the boys stand goose-pimpled
in football jerseys. Anything for a hug or kiss,
anything to be healed. A new-green leaf swells sap.
Each bud is a nose pressed against a windowpane,
a breast gazing through thin cotton. The cold stings,
& a shiver goes from crown to feet, leaf tip down to taproot.
The next-door boy's snowman bows to Monday's rush hour.
Heavy metal leaps from a car & ignites the spluttering air.
Each little tight fist of clutched brightness begins to open,
distant & close as ghost laughter in the afternoon.
A crow sits on the fence, telling me how many ways
to answer its brutal questions about tomorrow.
The season is a white buffalo birthing in the front yard:
big-eyed with beauty, half out & half in.
Branches cluster with mouths ready to speak
a second coming, & a wind off the Delaware

springs forth, rattling the window sashes.
An all-night howl slips beneath the eaves,
& next day, frozen buds are death's-heads
fallen into footprints coming & gone.

ECLOGUE AT MIDNIGHT

The creatures forged to guard us in sleep
climb down from their high portals
& huddle in lonely alleyways.
The gardens couldn't hold them
with natural or false benediction.
Our house cats become their Seeing Eye dogs,
& our noble dogs curl their tails
between their legs, bow their heads,
whine, & back away from silhouettes
moonlight casts along the walls.
We weren't born to love them
out of their classical horror,
though unlit amusement parks
are their playgrounds. They skid
down slides & spin on the merry-go-
rounds. They climb telephone poles
& walk power lines. They tiptoe up
to our bedroom windows & peep in.
Their presence lives next morning
in the office, in the barber's chair,
sipping black coffee from a paper cup
& reading annual reports at the desk.

Whatever silver tongue we pray in
they've learned to cajole & curse,
& grow beautiful when ridden
by the five shadows of Venus.

IGNIS FATUUS

Something or someone. A feeling
among a swish of reeds. A swampy
glow haloes the Spanish moss,
& there's a swaying at the edge
like a child's memory of abuse
growing flesh, living on what
a screech owl recalls. Nothing
but a presence that fills up
the mind, a replenished body
singing its way into double-talk.
In the city, "Will o' the Wisp"
floats out of Miles's trumpet,
leaning ghosts against nighttime's
backdrop of neon. A foolish fire
can also start this way: before
you slide the key into the lock
& half turn the knob, you know
someone has snuck into your life.
A high window, a corner of sky
spies on upturned drawers of underwear
& unanswered letters, on a tin box
of luminous buttons & subway tokens,
on books, magazines, & clothes

flung to the studio's floor,
his sweat still owning the air.
Years ago you followed someone
here, in love with breath
kissing the nape of your neck,
back when it was easy to be
at least two places at once.

THE STORY OF A COAT

We talked about Baroness Pannonica
driving her Silver Pigeon to the Five Spot
to chauffeur Monk home. I was happy
not to talk football, the inventory of skulls
in a cave in Somalia, the democratic vistas
of the Cedar Tavern, or about Spinoza.
We were saying how the legs go first,
& then from the eyes mystery is stolen.
I said how much I miss Bill Matthews,
that sometimes at the Village Vanguard,
Fez, or Smalls, especially when some cat
steals a riff out of Prez's left back pocket,
I hear his Cincinnati laugh. Then our gaze
snagged on a green dress shifting the light.
If you'd asked me, I couldn't have said why
I knew jasmine from the silence of Egypt,
or how water lives only to remember fire.
As we walked out of the sanctuary of garlic,
chive, onion, mushroom, & peppery dough,
we agreed Rahsaan could see rhythm
when he blew wounded cries of night hawks
at daybreak. The heat of the pizza parlor
followed us to the corner, & two steps later

I remembered the scent of loneliness
in my coat left draped over the chair.
I had fallen in love with its cut,
how it made me walk straighter.
When I passed the young James Dean
coming out the door with my blue-gray coat
balled up in his arms, I didn't stop him.
I don't know why. I just stood there
at the table. But, David, years after
I circled the globe, I'm still ashamed
of memories that make me American
as music made of harmony & malice.

TEN OR ELEVEN DISGUISES

I *Pretending to Be a Rock*

A twin of its long dreaming, this creature is its own god,
oxymoron & devilfish.

A chunk of broken-off reef self-love sinks into—unmoving, asleep
in the attitude of a stone.

The billowy gills working down there are its only belief system.
The rock ascends through a starry effusion.

The mouth is a question slowly opening its eyes,
& the answer turns the water red.

II *Shades*

She slips behind dark glasses,
but she isn't hiding a black eye
or bruise from the public.

She wants to stay there, half
hidden, anywhere else
other than where she is—

halfway through the door
of the Silk City Café,
around corners of a hard look.

Why can't they stop
trying to find lost selves
& outlaw galaxies?

They say, Damn!
Your eyes are so—
so beautiful & scary.

Is there a single word
that falls between blue
& silvery green? Hyacinth

eases out to the edge
of a cautious smile,
but never lasts longer than a year.

III *Blush*

The woman sitting across from me
on a train headed to the airport
clicks open her compact mirror
& brushes rouge on her nose & cheeks.

Does she know powder can't erase Africa
or the snip of an eyelid transform Asia?
Can she see our ancestor holding his little bow
& bone-tipped arrow to bring down a wildebeest

or wild boar easy as a lovetap?
She works the delicate brush to the edge
of a question, across her jawbone,
& now she's a face on a billboard overlooking a village,

a voice only when the projector dies.
She begs for a glimpse of the dead living
in a landscape between blue & doubt,
for a whole colony of eyes on her.

By tomorrow this time I'll be in Florence
singing to Leda of how a notorious heart
may own buttocks, root, & whimpering bud,
but underneath hides a masterpiece.

IV *Bleaching Cream*

She was wounded by a word
somewhere in the Third World.
The mirror now taunts her nightly,

saying, You are the Queen of Sheba
before her caravan rolled across desert sand,
before she dreamt of King Solomon's bed.

v *Metamorphosis*

I'm turning you into a girl
chasing a butterfly, a she-wolf
on a hilltop, & then back into a woman.

vi *Addendum to a Discourse*

You know, I love these juicy pears from China.
I think they ascend the trees & brush each bud
with a little feathery doo-dad. Yes, that's right.
They climb ladders & slowly bend branches
toward them, & then lightly brush the pollen
on opening blossoms. Just a slight touch.
When little fists appear, they wrap each one
in a papery gauze. They prop up woven nets
of mesh almost thin as breath to keep away birds,
& wait for ripening to unweave up through the roots.
Just bite into this one, & your tongue will remember
foreverness. But, darling, I don't know what this says
about global warming, why dead bees are in the honey
or fallen beside the hive's blustery swarmhole.

ODE TO THE CHAMELEON

Little shape shifter, lingering
there on your quotidian twig
of indifference, you are a glimpse
of a rainbow, your eyes an iota
of amber. If nature is mind,
it knows you are always
true, daring the human eye
to see deeper. You are envy
& solace approaching green,
no more than an eyeblink
in a corner of the Old World.
You are a tilt of the head
& vantage point, neither this
nor that, clearly prehistoric
& futuristic, & then you are
gone. In your little theater
of osmosis, you're almost
a piece of tropical work woven
from the alchemist's skin habit.
Called into the hanging garden,
you sit there, almost unseen
as dusky shadows climb
the blooming Judas tree.

A TRANSLATION OF SILK

One can shove his face against silk
& breathe in centuries of perfume
on the edge of a war-torn morning
where men fell so hard for iron
they could taste it. Now, today,
a breeze disturbs a leafy pagoda
printed on slow cloth. A creek
begins to move. His brain trails,
lagging behind his fingers to learn
suggestion is more than radiance
shaped to the memory of hands,
that one of the smallest creatures
knows how to be an impressive god.
A flounce of light is the only praise
it ever receives. I need to trust
this old way of teaching a man
to cry, & I want to believe in
what's left of the mulberry leaves.
Humans crave immortality, but oh,
yes, to think worms wove this
as a way to stay alive in our world.

ODE TO THE SHAKUHACHI

You call till the dead rise
with a flutter of the tongue,
crying & laughing in one note.
Five mouth holes—four in front
& one in back—you are octaves
cut into two feet of bamboo.
You are more than a tube
the brain tooled to incant
across the maddening abyss,
more than wind through leaves,
or oaths whispered to gods.
"The Sound of Deer Calling
to One Another" says each moan
is a credo begged through reed.
Your mind's naked weather
blows across the breath holes,
& Basho's *Narrow Road*
to the Deep North forks into
a familiar footpath. You say
everything never said before,
& daytime rises out of blood
the moon left on flagstone.
Listen closely. Hear every last,

slow, bold, quick sensation
shaken from writhing reed
a roguish heart may fix on.
You are a plea prying itself loose,
till there's the wet light of a wingtip.

THE ONE-HANDED CONCERTO

After Paul Wittgenstein
lost his right hand in the Great War,
he begged his friend Ravel
for a concerto of muted tom-toms
& peacock feathers underneath the tempo.
Something oceanic, with gusto & pulse
inside a refrain left on the battlefield.

Phantom fingers played the bridge
between ivory, allegory, & wood.
If the left hand can't forgive or forget
its brother, blood seeps from the song
when white bones peer out of earth.
He rehearsed the Concerto in D
till Pan & Beauty danced in a grove,

till he could lift a hem with a smile
& five knowing fingers on the keys.
Perhaps he could even forget & snap
the fingers of his lost hand to call his dog home,
& it would come running full trot, wagging its tail.
But he didn't know if he'd ever learn to play absence,
because he could cover only one ear.

Weeks later they stood at a window
gazing at an orange sunset when a grackle
flew into the glass & knocked itself crazy,
& that was when he first said, Okay,
I may have learned to articulate the silence of silk
falling, but I cannot teach my shadow to stop
limping three paces behind when I take a bow.

DEAD RECKONING

Fishermen follow a dream of the biggest
catch, out among the tall waves where
freshwater meets a salty calmness.
For hundreds of years they've crossed
this body of water, casting their nets
& singing old songs. They've slept
with the village women & ridden waves
back to the other side to loved ones.
Now, lost in the old clothes of unreason
& wanderlust, their nets sag with the last
of its kind, with bountiful fish stories,
& soon the flirtatious mermaids are
beckoning from a swoon of reeds,
calling their names. The first dance
is desire. The second dance is love.
The tall grass quivers like a siren
snagged in a shabby net. Now,
as if on a journey of lost souls,
love & desire dance with death,
twirling bright skirts till flesh & cloth
turn into ashes. What did they do
to make the gods angry? Forbidden
laughter of the mermaids fills the night,
& if humans try to sing this laughter,
their voices only cry out in the dark.

CAPE COAST CASTLE

I made love to you, & it loomed there.
We sat on the small veranda of the cottage,
& listened hours to the sea talk.
I didn't have to look up to see if it was still there.
For days, it followed us along polluted beaches
where the boys herded cows
& the girls danced for the boys,
to the money changer,
& then to the marketplace.
It went away when the ghost of my mother
found me sitting beneath a palm,
but was in the van with us on a road trip to the country
as we zoomed past thatch houses.
It was definitely there when a few dollars
exchanged hands & we were hurried
through customs, past the guards.
I was standing in the airport in Amsterdam,
sipping a glass of red wine, half lost in Van Gogh's
swarm of colors, & it was there, brooding in a corner.
I walked into the public toilet, thinking of W. E. B.
buried in a mausoleum, & all his books & papers
going to dust, & there it was, in that private moment,
the same image: obscene because it was built
to endure time, stronger than their houses & altars.
The seeds of melon. The seeds of gumbo in trade winds

headed to a new world. I walked back into the throng
of strangers, but it followed me. I could see the path
slaves traveled, & I knew when they first saw it
all their high gods knelt on the ground.
Why did I taste salt water in my mouth?
We stood in line for another plane,
& when the plane rose over the city
I knew it was there, crossing the Atlantic.
Not a feeling, but a longing. I was in Accra
again, gazing up at the vaulted cathedral ceiling
of the compound. I could see the ships at dusk
rising out of the lull of "Amazing Grace," cresting
the waves. The governor stood on his balcony,
holding a sword, pointing to a woman
in the courtyard, saying, That one.
Bring me that tall, ample wench.
Enslaved hands dragged her to the center,
then they threw buckets of water on her,
but she tried to fight. They pinned her to the ground.
She was crying. They prodded her up the stairs. One step,
& then another. Oh, yeah, she still had some fight in her,
but the governor's power was absolute. He said,
There's a tyranny of language in my fluted bones.
There's poetry on every page of the Good Book.
There's God's work to be done in a forsaken land.

There's a whole tribe in this one, but I'll break them
before they're in the womb, before they're conceived,
before they're even thought of. Come, up here,
don't be afraid, up here to the governor's quarters,
up here where laws are made. I haven't delivered
the head of Pompey or John the Baptist
on a big silver tray, but I own your past,
present, & future. You're special.
You're not like the others. Yes,
I'll break you with fists & cat-o'-nine.
I'll thoroughly break you, head to feet,
but, sister, I'll break you most dearly
with sweet words.

SAPPHO OF MYTILENE

You're always lying in bed
lonely as a stone in the mouth
of a river, clothed in moon glow
& slime weed. With Aphrodite

in mind & the heart's curvature,
she left her shape singing among lily
shoots & hairy tubers. Aeolic sighs
are carved in every fleshy question

& stone, with hold & release,
& the longing scent of prey
draws the huntress three steps
closer with each held breath.

Disrobed beneath Pleiades,
goosefleshed in your silken
sarcophagus, you still lust after
every mirror a reflection bathes in.

THE CAGE, THE HEAD

You sit inside a halved atlas.
Something for us to stare at
as you define us
by how long you hold a gaze.

You're swollen with wings
because we move around you.
Caught in an orbit of the frontal lobe,
neither right nor left, & of course,
that is your true number.

Someone says Mr. Blockhead,
but I call you Ms. Manifold.
You're slanted into a pose
& held to your base plate
by twelve bronze spikes,
& then beaten till you rise.

KINDNESS

When deeds splay before us
precious as gold & unused chances
stripped from the whine bone,
we know the moment kindheartedness
walks in. Each "praise be"
echoes us back as the years uncount
themselves, eating salt. Though blood
first shaped us on the climbing wheel,
the human mind lit by the savanna's
ice star & thistle rose,
your knowing gaze enters a room
& opens the day,
saying we were made for fun.
Even the bedazzled brute knows
when sunlight falls through leaves
across honed knives on the table.
If we can see it push shadows
aside, growing closer, are we less
broken? A barometer, temperature
gauge, a ruler in minus fractions
& pedigrees, a thingamajig,
a probe with an all-seeing eye,
what do we need to measure

every held breath & unkind leap year?
Sometimes a sober voice is enough
to calm the waters & drive away
the false witnesses, saying, Look,
here are the broken treaties Beauty
brought to us earthbound sentinels.

BLACK FIGS

Because they tasted so damn good, I swore
    I'd never eat another one, but three seedy little hearts
beckoned tonight from a green leaf-shaped saucer,
    swollen with ripeness, ready to spill a gutty
sacrament on my tongue. Their skins too smooth
    to trust or believe. Shall I play Nat King Cole's
"Nature Boy" or Cassandra's "Death Letter"
    this Gypsy hour? I have a few words to steal
back the taste of earth. I know laughter can rip
    stitches, & deeds come undone in the middle of a dance.
Socrates talked himself into raising the cup to his lips
    to toast the avenging oracle, but I told the gods no
false kisses, they could keep their ambrosia & nectar,
    & let me live my days & nights. I nibble each globe,
each succulent bud down to its broken-off stem
    like a boy trying to make a candy bar last
the whole day, & laughter unlocks my throat
    when a light falls across Bleecker Street
against the ugly fire escape.

AUBADE AT HOTEL COPERNICUS

I can still see your white blouse & black Gypsy skirt
with veins of pepper red running through it
in Warsaw, turning a corner in the eye
an hour before our fingers trace an inscription
on the house where Chopin's piano tumbled
from a window. As you speak I see a city
gutted by war & torn down to stone clouds,
then rising in an Italian painter's drawings.
Did the shuffled blueprints recast the sky?
Next morning, exiled between the eighth
& ninth circles, the train outruns the rakish
yellow fields uncoiling. Did we talk about
how California light melted the crystal rib
of earth in Milosz's poetry, & did we wish
for his translations of the spirituals as a bridge
back to the true man? Upturned soil shines
among naked roots. Each question is an eye
begging for its hook. I slowly turn away
from you. Running trees & windowpanes
flash quickly as a dead man's deck of cards.
But when I open my eyes, another beauty
pierces my heart. A medieval light falls
on the buildings. How many lamentations
bounced off these walls & kept traveling

beyond? I know this is how place & time
own humans. Copernicus's heavenly bodies
guide us along cobblestones up to the castle
& down to the river, into the dragon's cave,
through the Tuscan cul-de-sacs where
blue begins. How many ghosts followed us
into the basement to Muniak's bebop gig
to hear the saxophone argue with the piano?
A blade of grass in a bottle made me sing
& count footsteps to the hotel. Of course,
we knew we'd face the heavy wooden doors
guarding other tales. We knock till the clerk
spies through a peep & uncouples the latch,
& hand in hand, we enter to be strummed
till mercy unfolds torn wings in the dark,
till the forsaken heals. We have no vows
or oaths to mend the tongue, but something says
this isn't the time to remember Galileo's trial.
A sparrow or a lark seeks refuge in the rafters,
promising us the night's thirsty rapture.
If there's blood in a stone, we shall find it.
If there's sugar in fruit, an ant trail will cross
our threshold. The waning moon is Sagittarius.
The arrow is out of its quiver, & we know the sun
will bring bees at dawn to work the poppies.

FATA MORGANA

I could see thatch boats. The sea
swayed against falling sky. Mongolian
horses crested hills, helmets edging the perimeter,
& I saw etched on the horizon scarab insignias.
The clangor of swords & armor echoed
& frightened scorpions into their holes,
& the question of zero clouded the brain.
I saw three faces of my death foretold.
I sat at a table overflowing with muscadine & quince,
but never knew a jealous husband poisoned the Shiraz.
I laughed at his old silly joke about Caligula
lounging in a bathhouse made of salt blocks.
I was on a lost ship near the equator,
& only a handful of us were still alive,
cannibal judgment in our eyes.
I came to a restful valley of goats & dragon lizards,
but only thought of sand spilling from my boots.
I witnessed the burning of heretics near an oasis,
& dreamt of gulls interrogating sea horses, cuttlefish,
& crabs crawling out of the white dunes.
I could see the queen of scapegoats
donning a mask as palms skirted the valley.
I was lost in a very old land, before Christ

& Muhammad, & when I opened my eyes
I could see women embracing a tribunal
of gasoline cans. I heard a scuttling
on the seafloor. I knew beforehand
what surrender would look like after
long victory parades & proclamations,
& could hear the sounds lovemaking
brought to the cave & headquarters.

CONCEIVED IN A TIME OF WAR

Because your mother & father kissed
beneath a hail of Roman candles,
you crawled out of one thousand
tiny deaths, stubborn as aster
in stony clay. A goddess of dawn
scooted under a zing of barbed wire
to witness your birth. After three moans
& nine months you were here, a squiggle
across a breathing map. Terror & joy
dragged up tinged cries of Eurydice
from a starlit bunker. Morphine
transfigured days of sirens till only
an afterglow lives in night's shattered
corner. You have a Paleolithic brain
shaped by talk of glory & anthems.
Your cry is several broken treaties.
Your mind is a scrap of sailcloth
& a wishbone, a theory of perfect
flight. Here's a thimble of wine
& paper-thin bread as a welcoming
toast. You were born to know hell,
but you shouldn't lose precious sleep
over a soul buzzing around a wormhole
eaten into the season's last bruised pear.

MEMORY OF THE MURDERED PROFESSORS AT THE JAGIELLONIAN

—AFTER HASIOR

They fired a bullet into the head
of each question, trying to kill Kant's
unending argument with Hegel.
They burned laws, moral codes,
& the Golden Mean. Anyone
serving tea & cookies to Death,
looking or acting as if he knew love,
stood before the firing squad.
All questions had to go. Pronoun
or noun. If it crawled on busted kneecaps,
whimpering & begging for mercy,
it was still half of a question.

∎

The little skyscraper of glass boxes
sunlight strikes the same time of day
at a certain angle outside Zakopane

looks like condos where nimble ghosts
still stand up to the darkest answers.
No, I can't hear one voice pleading.
But I do hear gusts coming down
from the hills. No, you're wrong again.
The crow perched on the totem is real.
Look at how the light lifts off its wings,
but I wish I could understand what it is
he's trying to say. I think I heard a name.

ENGLISH

When I was a boy, he says, the sky began burning,
& someone ran knocking on our door
one night. The house became birds
in the eaves too low for a boy's ears.

I heard a girl talking, but they weren't words.
I knew one good thing: a girl
was somewhere in our house,
speaking slow as a sailor's parrot.

I glimpsed Alice in Wonderland.
Her voice smelled like an orange,
though I'd never peeled an orange.
I knocked on the walls, in a circle.

The voice was almost America.
My ears plucked a word out of the air.
She said, Friend. I eased open the door
hidden behind overcoats in a closet.

The young woman was smiling at me.
She was teaching herself a language
to take her far, far away,
& she taught me a word each day to keep secret.

But one night I woke to other voices in the house.
A commotion downstairs & a pleading.
There are promises made at night
that turn into stones at daybreak.

From my window, I saw the stars
burning in the river brighter than a big
celebration. I waited for her return,
with my hands over my mouth.

I can't say her name, because it was
dangerous in our house so close to the water.
Was she a boy's make-believe friend
or a beehive breathing inside the walls?

Years later my aunts said two German soldiers
shot the girl one night beside the Vistula.
This is how I learned your language.
It was long ago. It was springtime.

POPPIES

These frantic blooms can hold their own
when it comes to metaphor & God.
Take any name or shade of irony, any flowery
indifference or stolen gratitude, & our eyes,
good or bad, still run up to this hue.
Take this woman sitting beside me,

a descendant of Hungarian Gypsies
born to teach horses to dance & eat sugar
from her hand, does she know beauty
couldn't have protected her, that a poppy
tucked in her hair couldn't have saved her
from those German storm troopers?

This frightens me. I see eyes peeping
through narrow slats of cattle cars
hurrying toward forever. I see "Jude"
& "Star of David" scribbled across a depot,
but she says, That's the name of a soccer team,
baby. Red climbs the hills & descends,

hurrying out to the edge of a perfect view,
& then another, between white & violet.
It is a skirt or cape flung to the ground.
It is old denial worked into the soil.
It is a hungry new vanity that rises
& then runs up to our bleating train.

I am a black man, a poet, a bohemian,
& there isn't a road my mind doesn't travel.
I also have my cheap, one-way ticket
to Auschwitz & know of no street or footpath
death hasn't taken. The poppies rush ahead,
up to a cardinal singing on barbed wire.

ORPHEUS AT THE
SECOND GATE OF HADES

My lyre has fallen & broken,
but I have my little tom-toms.
Look, do you see those crows
perched on the guardhouse?
I don't wish to speak of omens,
but sometimes it's hard to guess.
Life has been good the past few years.
I know all seven songs of the sparrow,
& I feel lucky to be alive. I woke up at 2:59
this morning reprieved because I fought
dream catchers & won. I'll place a stone
into my mouth & go down there again,
& if I meet myself mounting the stairs
it won't be the same man descending.
Doubt has walked me to the river's edge
before. I may be ashamed, but I can't forget
how to mourn & praise on the marimba.
I shall play till the day's golden machinery
stops between the known & unknown.
The place was a funeral pyre for the young

who died before knowing the thirst of man
or woman. Furies with snakes in their hair
wept. Tantalus ate pears & sipped wine
in a dream, as the eyes of a vulture
poised over Tityus' liver. I could see
Ixion strapped to a gyrating wheel
& Sisyphus sat on his rounded stone.
I shall stand again before Proserpine
& King Pluto. When it comes to defending love,
I can make a lyre drag down the moon & stars
but it's still hard to talk of earthly things—
ordinary men killing ordinary men,
women, & children. I don't remember
exactly what I said at the ticket office
my first visit here, but I do know it grew
ugly. The classical allusions didn't
make it any easier. I played a tune
that worked its way into my muscles,
& I knew I had to speak of what I'd seen
before the serpent drew back its head.
I saw a stall filled with human things, an endless
list of names, a hill of shoes, a room of suitcases
tagged to nowhere, eyeglasses, toothbrushes,
baby shoes, dentures, ads for holiday spas,

& a wide roll of thick cloth woven of living hair.
If I never possessed these reed flutes
& drums, if my shadow stops kissing me
because of what I have witnessed,
I shall holler to you through my bones,
I promise you.

THREE FIGURES AT THE
BASE OF A CRUCIFIXION

—AFTER FRANCIS BACON

Look how each pound of meat
manages to climb up & weigh itself
in the wobbly cage of the head.
Did the painter ascend a dogwood
or crawl into the hold of a slave ship
to get a good view of the thing
turning itself inside out beneath
a century of interrogation lamps?

It was always here, hiding behind
gauze, myth, doubt, blood, & spit.
After the exhibit on New Bond Street
they walked blocks around a garden
of April roses, tiger lilies, duckweed,
& trillium, shaking their heads.
The burning of mad silence left
powder rooms & tea parlors smoky.

Brushstrokes formed a blade to cut
the hues. A slipped disk
grew into a counterweight,
& the muse kept saying,
Learn to be kind to yourself.
A twisted globe of flesh
is held together by what
it pushes against.

A VISIT TO INNER SANCTUM

A poet stands on the steps of the great cathedral,
wondering if he has been a coward in hard times.
He traveled east, north, south, & seven directions
of the west. When he first arrived on the other side
of the sea, before he fell into the flung-open arms
of a long romance, the lemon trees were in bloom.

After a year, poised on the rift of a purple haze,
he forgot all the questions he brought with him.
Couldn't he see the tear gas drifting over Ohio
as flower children danced to Jefferson Airplane?
Will he ever write a sonnet dedicated to the memory
of four girls dynamited in a Birmingham church?

Standing in the cathedral again, in the midst
of what first calibrated his tongue —gold icons
& hidden jaguars etched into the high beams—
he remembers an emanation almost forgotten.
He can't stop counting dead heroes who lived in his head,
sultry refrains that kept him alive in the country of clouds.

Underneath the granite floor where he stands
loom the stone buttresses of an ancient temple.
When he was a boy, with his head bowed

close to the scarred floor, he could hear voices
rising from below, their old lingua franca
binding with his. How could he forget?

Outside the Institute of National Memory
he toasts the gods hiding between stanzas.
The girl he left behind for enemy soldiers
to rough up & frighten, she never stopped
waiting for him, even after she lost herself
in booze. Now he faces a rusty iron gate.

Did she know someday he'd question a life
till he held only a bone at the dull green door
of an icehouse where they stole their first kiss?
To have laughed beside another sweetheart
in a distant land is to have betrayed the soil
of dispossession hidden under his fingernails.

Supposed he'd pursued other, smaller passions
singing of night dew? The dead ones kept him
almost honest, tangoing with wives of despots
entranced by stolen light in his eyes & hair.
He never wanted to believe a pinch of salt
for a pinch of sugar is how scales are balanced.

THE SHORTEST NIGHT

I went into the forest searching
for fire inside pleading wood,
but I can't say for how long
I was moored between worlds.
I heard a magpie's rumination,
but I don't know if its wings
lifted the moon or let it drift
slow as a little straw boat
set ablaze on a winding river.
I learned the yellow-eyed wolf
is a dog & a man. A small boy
with a star pinned to his sleeve
was hiding among thornbushes,
or it was how the restless dark
wounded the pale linden tree
outside a Warsaw apartment.
Night crawls under each stone
quick as a cry held in the throat.
All I remember is my left hand
was holding your right breast
when I forced my eyes shut.
Then I could hear something
in the room, magnanimous

but small, half outside & half
inside, no more than a song—
an insomniac's one prophecy
pressed against the curtains,
forcing the ferns to bloom.

UNLIKELY CLAIMS

This is my house. My sweat is in the mortar
& hewn wood. This garden of garlic blooms
is mine too, said last night's pale ghost.
I know every crack where cold & light
try to sneak in, & where the past tongues
& grooves the future. I own every rusty nail.
This fence wasn't here when hobnailed boots
marched us into the night. I remember all
the cat-eye marbles would roll to this corner
of the kitchen. This tree limb my uncle cut
to make a witching rod. Here's the mark
an anniversary candle left on the counter,
said the ghost, slowly fingering
the deep burn like an old wound.
Now dirt-bike trails crisscross
the apple grove my father planted.
The goat tied beside the back gate
belongs to my progeny of beautiful
goats. You sold the mineral rights
under our feet, but the bird we hear
singing overhead in a Yiddish accent
owns the morning. These roses are mine
because I've walked through fire.

Go & tell your drinking buddies
& psychoanalyst your neighbor
has risen from the ashes. I wonder
if I should tell you about the love letters
hidden behind the doorjamb. This house
still stands among my lavender flowers.
Tell your inheritors to think of me
when they smile up at the sky.

WHEN EYES ARE ON ME

I am a scrappy old lion
who's wandered into a Christian square
quavering with centuries of forged bells.
The cobblestones make my feet ache.

I walk big-shouldered, my head raised
proudly. I smell the blood of a king.
The citizens can see only a minotaur in a maze.
I know more than a lion should know.

My roar goes back to the Serengeti,
to when a savanna was craggy ice,
but now it frightens only pigeons from a city stoop.
They believe they know my brain's contours & grammar.

Don't ask me how I know the signs engraved
on a sundial, the secret icons behind a gaze.
I wish their crimes hadn't followed me here.
I can hear their applause in the dusty citadel.

I know what it took to master the serpent
& wheel, the crossbow & spinal tap.
Once I was a leopard beside a stone gate.
I am a riddle to be unraveled. I am not

& I am. When their eyes are on me
I become whatever is judged badly.
I circle the park. Hunger shapes
my keen sense of smell, a lifetime ahead.

They will follow my pawprints
till they're lost in snow at dusk.
If I walk in circles, I hide from my shadow.
They plot stars to know where to find me.

I am a prodigal bird perched on the peak
of a guardhouse. I have a message
for fate. The sunlight has shown me
the guns, & their beautiful sons are deadly.

BLACKBIRDING ON THE HUDSON

Great river, you've journeyed a long way to find me here in
    Czestochowa
  this morning. I reached up to grab a book from a crowded shelf,
& my unwilled fingers opened the pages to "The Mouth of the
    Hudson."
  Perhaps omens speak more clearly across a desert or the sea.
A blood-hold is in language, & water connects us to what we are
    made of
  as rain falls outside. The way a river drives a long path home,
over the rocky years, going around & through rough earth, around
    edges of other worlds, I have also gone where love has taken me.
I still believe water is memory. It is true. I know the trees remind
    rivers
  of where they've journeyed, & their rings have something to
    do with
sundials & clocks made of stone. The hawk circling in my mind,
    overhead
  at this moment, is a merciless hypnosis over your unwinding
    surface,
& one bird devours another bird in midair. Although I'm not the
    bird-watcher
  in Lowell's poem, with a good eye trained on the cobalt blue
    horizon,

I do know something about coke fumes & the chemical air of
     New Jersey.
     But there's another phrase—I think it is "blackbirding"—
          pecking fiercely
at my gut. Body of resolve, body of water, do you know anything
     about this?
     Though Minerva sat on her classic sunlit throne, she didn't
          condemn
or condone the heart's industry & skulduggery in your timeless
     wanderlust,
     & savage deeds breached her limestone stare at the port of
          no return.
I'd love to forget those years when a black boy or girl sent to the
     grocery store
     at dusk to buy a loaf of bread, or three red apples, or a quart
          of kerosene,
or a half pound of salt meat could disappear between a laugh &
     a cry
     as you pretended to be River Styx. Where are we going, mister?
Hogtied down in boats, gagged or conked over the head, boys
     & girls
     cried out for mothers & fathers, to God. At what hour of the
          night
the blood remembers that first voyage in the hold across the
     Atlantic?

They rode out those tossing storms in cotton fields & canebrakes
of the Deep South. There are as many views of you as there are
          stations along
     the way, carving out your reach & plunge. River, though it's
     day here
& nighttime there, keep speaking to me. Beauty can't set records
          straight,
     though you're praised in songs, a fortress of light through
     cattails
dredging up everything you know. Native Americans parted your
          bosom
     with canoes, riding out your wildness, trawling for bass & shad,
before others gutted you. Heir to birch & false orchid, you're a
          tough one,
     moving over rocks, carving your way night & day, hundreds
     left reeling
in your grip. When I hear Thelonious Monk's "Coming on the
          Hudson,"
     I think of the kidnapped who believed they could walk on water,
as their captors cursed each other for losing their precious, sacked,
     breathing cargo. I know the mockingbird stole cries out of
     the air,
passed them down through the egg, & is now our only reliable
          witness.

BEGOTTEN

I'm the son of poor Mildred & illiterate J.W.
But I sit here with Ninun's song in my mouth,
knowing the fantastic blue Bull of Heaven
because I've cried at a woman's midnight door
clouded by sea mist. Grief followed me, saying,
Burn your keepsakes, or give them to Goodwill
or the Salvation Army, & then live on the streets.
But I couldn't forget a half-dead, ugly prickly pear
breaking into twenty-three yellow blooms.
Namtar's bird of prey perched on my shoulder
as I wandered darkness searching for light,
knowing, finally, I was born to be hooked
quickly as a fish. To spend an hour in Uruk
tonight is to awake in the Green Zone
with another dictator's lassoed statue
pulled to the ground. The gods count
the dead, running eyes over folly, guilt,
& restitution, saying, Now, dear one,
you are bread. They tally grain & stock
noted in cuneiform, & I hear a whisper:
Bread for Neti, the keeper of the gate,
bread for Ningizzida, the serpent god
& fat lord of the ever-living tree,

& bread for Enmul, bread for all of them.
We dream of going from one desire
to the next. But in the final analysis,
a good thought is the simplest food.
Ninhursag is the mother of creation,
& the ants her most trustful servants
because they are always on their way.

BLUE DEMENTIA

In the days when a man
would hold a swarm of words
inside his belly, nestled
against his spleen, singing.

In the days of night riders
when life tongued a reed
till blues & sorrow song
called out of the deep night:
Another man done gone.
Another man done gone.

In the days when one could lose oneself
all up inside love that way,
& then moan on the bone
till the gods cried out in someone's sleep.

Today,
already I've seen three dark-skinned men
discussing the weather with demons
& angels, gazing up at the clouds
& squinting down into iron grates
along the fast streets of luminous encounters.

I double-check my reflection in plate glass
& wonder, Am I passing another
Lucky Thompson or Marion Brown
cornered by a blue dementia,
another dark-skinned man
who woke up dreaming one morning
& then walked out of himself
dreaming? Did this one dare
to step on a crack in the sidewalk,
to turn a midnight corner & never come back
whole, or did he try to stare down a look
that shoved a blade into his heart?
I mean, I also know something
about night riders & catgut. Yeah,
honey, I know something about talking with ghosts.

A POEM WRITTEN INSIDE
A BIG ROUND MACHINE

Because I could hear a deep hum of radiant gears
    uncoupling & locking— though my ears were muffled—
I couldn't believe the sound of eternity droning in my head,
    & it was then the big round machine began to speak.
Breathe in. Breathe out. Breathe in, & hold your breath.
    A black horse galloped across an endless white field.
Trees were marching. Tectonic plates began to shift
    under what I know. How did Billie's voice find me?
Breathe out. Here's a young Marguerite Duras
    beckoning me into her lovely outstretched arms.
Yes, it's a good thing the boat from France
    is coming to take her away . . . How did they know
when to send in the clowns? Now, that's Ornette
    Live at Prince Street. For a moment, I dozed off,
but I'd know his sound anywhere. The day moved back
    & forth on a beam of light. Someone leaned over
to kiss me. Since I once loved sugar, a rainbow
    is in my head because in my back teeth
there's now a bittersweet horde of gold.

FORTUNE

Once upon a time, she'd glide down Fifth Avenue
decked out in a mink coat, but Andrea Mantegna
hadn't captured a hint of her perfume.
All the would-be queens for half a day
seemed to adore her fat pearls.
Our hearts strolled at the same rhythm
she strolled. A crescent moon tarried
beside the north star, as if illuminating a catwalk.
Brandishing laurel & thorns, we were her virtues
& vices. No, I can't say if her eyes were green
or blue, or lit by a silk road of frankincense
& myrrh. Mercury & Pan were on their way
to the graveyard shift, traversing trapdoors
along the sidewalk. How were we to know
if our gaze wasn't on her, she couldn't live?

FLESH

You wish to know if I cherished a thought
    beyond lore & decorum, if a bloodless virtue
like some fury of wings beating in a cage
    ushered me beyond paradise. Unbelievable
as I am, I shall say this: if I am Beatrice
    or Beatitude, muse or pale siren, I am flesh
born to another dream of flesh. If I am clay,
    it is the same merciless clay you are made of,
with a red vein of iron running through it, the same
    naked prayer in the dark holding the song together.

The one who tried to raise me above the laws
    of Nature & praise me into unearthly perfection
was my brother's friend, who called Love his master,
    & I can remember the first time his eyes
strained to unlock the lonely temple of my bones:
    we were both nine years old, reposed in the day's
scripture. Attired in crimson lighter than breath
    & memory, I daydreamed of my wooden dolls
asleep in identical beds, cast into a world of reason.
    It was not a Sabbath divided by three.

I inherited the Virgin Mary's guarded gaze
    & smile. As the years passed, I knew nine

was its own circle as I crossed cobblestones
    between my two chaperons. That day
I spoke his name at the edge of a sigh,
    I did not know I was entering a ledger
of remembrance, & did not wish to be
    a woman purely rhymed out of words.
When Love mastered my creator, Love was
    a man or phantom, but I was born Beatrice.

Did my red hair & pale skin make me angelic
    in a country of raven hair? My creator
wrote down every white bone in my body,
    but he did not know the right questions
to summon me to desire. He did not know
    nobility seldom resides in the noble,
that gold or silver always finds a way to work
    itself out of the black earth, to force
the sun to make it dance in the air.
    He did not know I hurt to know.

I love sun & rain on my skin. My suitor
    & conjurer, is that the burden, the curse,
the gift? Does wisdom make my eyelashes
    tremble, does it draw the blood forth, unearth
temptation? When innocence measured me
    from crown to a dancer's arch, the Furies

marked my path. He said my name,
    & the day turned to gulls crying—stolen
out of his mouth & put back into mine.
    I am my own communion wine & bread.

I am the lost breath of medieval desire,
    but not a false image, a sonnet, a canzone,
or a hidden metaphor. Let me measure
    an unrhymed lament along the path
into the trees. If I am wrong or outdistanced,
    if I lose my way or marry a banker's son,
then let the sunlight undermine my stride
    as a vein of pleasure unties my body
& unholy mind from the firmament,
    its fiery lessons written in his master text.

Though my family name bequeathed me
    to a rich man & I ate only sugared almonds
on my wedding day, I trust a bird cried
    nightlong on the bedroom windowsill.
The one who shaped me from the vernacular
    sang also of harmony, but I wished for Love
to speak to me as a human being out of Ovid,
    from the blood of birth & death. I was happy
a whisper finally shook my heart awake
    in this city of beautiful desolation.

Imbued with shame? How can we deny
    a rose its thorns? I wish an infidelity
of memory, if human means not to know shame
      & guilt in the worm-eaten afterworld.
Because there is neither a sweet style
    nor truth in purest white. I crave the dark bread
of Tuscany & sun-ripened figs. God did not wound me
    with pity, but made me to love beyond reason
& to know the salt of tears, to pray & defecate,
      & to stand reflected by the clear waters of the Arno.

I was made to praise the winter sparrow
    on its naked branch. My creator's eyes
failed to reach into the ultimate question,
    into the marrow & laughter, into the sorrow
& doubt. He & his old river of words—
    I came to myself on the bank of Lethe,
lost in chance, carried by a desirous wing.
    My last garment had fallen to the ground,
& a battered angel entrusted me her credence.
    I walked behind mystery's first sister.

I was not numerology or philosophy. Because
    my creator could not imagine me as a woman
in his arms, he dreamt me an early death
    in his head. The word made mythical.

My name grew into a sonata he learned
    to put back into his mouth, an echo
of his voice in the wind. My blood seethed
    into his words, an immaculate conception
in reverse, & no one could keep God's worms
    out of the tomb after I died in childbirth.

GRUNGE

No, sweetheart, I said *courtly love*.
I was thinking of John Donne's
"Yet this enjoys before it woo,"
but my big hands were dreaming
Pinetop's boogie-woogie piano
taking the ubiquitous night apart.
Not Courtney. I know "inflated tear"
means worlds approaching pain
& colliding, or a heavenly body
calling to darkness, & that shame
has never been my truest garment,
because I was born afraid of needles.
But I've been shoved up against
frayed ropes too, & I had to learn
to bob & weave, to duck & hook,
till I could jab my way out of
a foregone conclusion, till blues
reddened a room. All I know is,
sometimes a man wants only a hug
when something two-steps him
toward a little makeshift stage.
Somehow, between hellhounds
& a guitar solo made of gutstring
& wood, I outlived a stormy night
with snow on my eyelids.

NOSTALGIA, OR
BETWEEN LOVERS

While the east slept in the arms of the west
each house broke into two divided houses,
& concertina rolled out across dead of night
& cleaved a full moon. Doors were nailed shut
between the two. We stood days at a window
watching soldiers march up & down till blocks
settled into the mortar, propped against
philosophy & slant, temple door & curfew.
The bird emissaries flew higher. The mole
burrowed deeper. Seven crows called
from the windowsill: What's a wall for?
I said, To keep out. To hem in. To hold
in place till there are no more crimes
of passion left in the world. In this room
only drunken dancing bears celebrated.
These walls held all the smallest secrets.
Here's where loving owned the night,
& of course, bread was also broken.
In this living room, *Dallas*, *Jeopardy*,
& *Falcon Crest* made the darkness kneel.
Up here among rafters someone trained

a covey of homing pigeons to fly love notes
to the other side. Did he know he'd pay
dearly for those sentimental infractions?
But he now swears he misses the old days,
that he needs something to push against
to hold himself together. I tell him, Look,
you're a lucky fool. I make a smart living
as a tour guide. If they hand over cold cash
for chunks of a fake wall, I'm here to please.
Did animals follow masters as they scaled
the wall to smoke reefer & play rock 'n' roll?
When it's raining on one side of the street
& the sun's shining on the other,
they say the devil's beating his wife.
Let's not speak of official good & evil,
but of a man & woman spooning bodies,
knowing what it takes to make love
go through gray concrete brightly.

GREEN

I've known billy club, tear gas, & cattle prod,
but not Black Sheep killing White Sheep.
Or vice versa. I've known water hoses
& the subterranean cry of a Black Maria
rounding a city corner on two angry wheels,
but couldn't smell cedar taking root in the air.

I've known of secret graves guarded
by the night owl in oak & poplar.
I've known police dogs on choke chains.
I've known how "We Shall Overcome"
feels on a half-broken tongue,
but not how deeply sunsets wounded the Peacock Throne.

Because of what I never dreamt
I know Hafez's litany balanced on Tamerlane's saber,
a gholam's song limping up the Elburz Mountains—
no, let's come back first to *now*,
to a surge of voices shouting,
Death to the government of potato!

Back to the iron horses of the Basijis
galloping through days whipped bloody
& beaten back into the brain's cave
louder than a swarm of percussion
clobbered in Enghelab Square,
cries bullied into alleyways & cutoffs.

Though each struck bell goes on
mumbling in the executioner's sleep,
there are always two hands holding
on to earth, & I believe their faith
in tomorrow's million green flags waving
could hold back a mile of tanks & turn

the Revolutionary Guard into stone,
that wherever a clue dares to step
a seed is pressed into damp soil.
A shoot, a tendril, the tip of a wing.
One breath at a time, it holds till it is
uprooted, or torn from its own grip.

DANGEROUSNESS

The neighbor's mask of Torquemada
says, I accuse you of whistling the radio's
aloneness a long way from Miami.
I press a drinking glass to the wall
between us, but you're reading Rimbaud
& other Romantics of the secret handshake
& scepter stealing the light of Havana.
You sit there as if you're the last living heir
of a mob boss, swearing you can't hear cries
from Guantánamo Bay, only a lost seagull
calling at dusk. Now, say all you know
about sweat & bedlam in the canefields,
how color works here. Trees are my eyes & ears,
& they accuse you of dangerousness, of laughing
at Che's ghost in the old Cathedral Square.
The waves carry your voice to the other side,
corrupting dolphin, electric eel, & starfish.
Forget the Bay of Pigs, the embargo,
abandoned ships & planes in a nightmare,
but you can't deny a hunger strike or No
rising out of the earth, a mind clouded
by monarchs lifting over the valley,
another man broken into a country.

I'll take the Buena Vista Social Club
over your damn blogosphere any day.
I accuse you of not knowing a son is a naked
solo, a song, a falsetto held till it draws blood.
Yes comes out of the ground through a reed.
I accuse you of falling for the sweetness
in pears, thinking you're so handsome.

THE WHITE DOG SYNDROME

The fluffy white dog sits on a throne of suitcases
stacked on the woman's luggage cart,

& her long black hair sways over the animal's pale eyes
as she uncaps a bottle of mineral water.

Her husband steps to the side & turns his back to them.
She dabs droplets of water off

the dog's mouth with a yellow tea towel & kisses it again.
I glimpse the whitish, ghostly figures

in the paintings I saw yesterday on the high walls of Siena,
the powdered faces of the rich

in a country of medieval peasants & no mercy in the sunlight.
I think of art & money.

The illuminated manuscripts slump
in their gold & pallor.

At least one hundred wings lift the day's heft, & white knights
astride fiery albino horses

gallop out of the Führer's exhibition. Curator of illusions,
pity the little dog she calls Caesar.

ODE TO THE GUITAR

The strings tremble & traverse
back up through that other
strong muscle singing blood
& guilt. Press a finger down,
& the message changes into blame
& beauty, into the scent of a garden
rising from peat moss & brimstone . . .
the frets & shaped neck worked
& caressed into a phantom limb
of hope. Does it have anything to do
with how the player's shoulder blades
curve out as if bowing over an altar
or how the doors of day & night
spring open, made to bridge
differences? Chance is fretted
till love moans swell in a gourd
hanging on an unknotted vine.
The strings hum inside stone,
undoing all the bright hooks
of promise stitched into silk
& printed cloth. Each note
true as a bone turning to dust,
suspended like an old belief

blooming from hush & blues
cries on the horizon. Catgut
& wood breathe together till
there's a beckoning left
quivering in the dark.

THE HEDONIST

I pull on my crow mask.
Butterflies & insects rise
in the ether of remembrance.
I suck all the sappy nectar
from honeysuckle blossoms
fallen in last night's scuffle
between gods & human shadows.

I'd die for October's last juicy plums
beside the shady marsh at the brink.
I'd stand on an anthill to learn
the blue heron's treatise on agony.
Every joy & sorrow are mine.
I bow to kiss a whipping post
so I can taste salt & contrition.

I know all the monsters lurking
in Lord Byron's verses. I follow
beauties up & down Broadway
till their masks own me.
I walk through the city,
saying, What did Kierkegaard know
about love & the God-worm?

After eating quail eggs & fish tongues,
I don a snarling dog mask
& pursue a would-be lover
into the hanging garden
till the Lethe is on her left
& the Styx is on her right,
& then I enter the labyrinth.

My alter ego is my servant.
Bring me fat gooseberries.
Translucent snails in sea salt.
Bring me a bit of Philopator's heart.
I have a taste for the fugu fish
because there's nothing
delicious as chance.

I've stood at a window
overlooking the Ideal City,
mouthing odes to a burnt silver spoon,
to a candle's flame-glut,
to a woman in the distance,
to the insipid angel
on the tip of a needle.

My caul has bitten into me.
I know the eternal earthworm.

Behind my peacock mask,
facing the Asiatic Sea,
I wonder what it would feel like
to follow pearl divers down, to know
the holy pressure of falling water.

HOW IT IS

My muse is holding me prisoner.
She refuses to give back my shadow,
anything that clings to a stone or tree
to keep me here. I recite dead poets
to her, & their words heal the cold air.
I feed her fat, sweet, juicy grapes,
& melons holding a tropical sun
inside them. From here, I see only
the river. The blue heron dives,
& always rises with a bright fish
in its beak, dangling a grace note.
She leans over & whispers, Someday,
I'll find some way to make you cry.
What are her three beautiful faces
telling me? I peel her an orange.
Each slice bleeds open a sigh.
Honeydew perfumes an evening
of black lace & torch songs,
& I bow down inside myself
& walk on my hands & knees
to break our embrace, but can't
escape. I think she knows
I could free myself of the thin gold chain

invisible around her waist,
but if she left the door open,
I'd still be standing here
in her ravenous light.
Her touch is alchemical.
When she questions my love,
I serve her robin's eggs
on a blue plate. She looks me in the eye
& says, You still can't go. Somehow,
I'd forgotten I'm her prisoner,
but I glance over at the big rock
wedged against the back door.
I think she knows, with her kisses
in my mouth, I could walk on water.

NIGHTTIME BEGINS WITH A LINE BY PABLO NERUDA

So my body went on growing, by night,
went on pleading & singing to the earth
I was born to be woven back into: Love,
let me see if I can't sink my roots
deeper into you, your minerals & water,
your leaf rot & gold, your telling & un-
telling of the oldest tales inscribed
on wind-carved rocks, silt & grass,
your songs & prayers, your oaths & myths,
your nights & days in one unending lament,
your luminous swarm of wet kisses
& stings, your spleen & mind,
your outrageous forgetting & remembrance,
your ghosts & rebirths, your thunderstones
& mushrooms, & your kind loss of memory.

SURRENDER

No, not again. I have to call Son House,
Ma Rainey, Leadbelly, Robert Johnson's
hellhounds to remind me of hairpin turns
in the false labyrinth. The twelve doors
of consolation have been flung wide open
before a thorny field of bloodred blossoms.
Somebody, some naked Ishtar of fusion
& war, please tell me I am addle-headed
as Caliban's sleepwalking apprentice.

Let me listen to Bud's "B-Flat Blues"
to see if the day can win itself back,
to see if I can endure this chink
in the breastplate, if this black clock
still knows anything about the busted
old knuckles of love & desire.
The brain's manifold mutates till
good is soaked with shit & blood,
born with a claw in its mouth.

I have stood up for the beautiful
hours of unreason & heartache,
but it was an old Sam Cooke

tune, "You Send Me,"
that wedded me to perchance.
Now I am on my stupid knees
before the love-rumpled bed,
begging a wing-footed goddess
to untie my hands & enter a simple plea on my behalf.

DAYBREAK

Succubus crawls out of his bed.
The infamous mask goes back
into its rosewood box,
& the lacquered lid with red roses
snaps shut. The new skin
of reason grows over doubt
again. The chicken snake angles up
from its hole, drawn to the same hint
of sun that opens the rooster's beak.
An oath bleeds through torn black silk.
Someone unties a prisoner's blindfold,
& somewhere a turtle's one eye blinks open.

How can the moon still be in the sky?
How does love live past this U-turn
in a city's wild heart? Somewhere
the lioness lifts her great paw,
& the gazelle rises. Then
she bounds past the watering hole,
into a yellowing ticket, a circle,
into the interior of a man's dream.
He can almost hear someone praying
to get even with his own reflection.
The alarm clock plays "Skylark,"
& the pain in the man's left side goes away.

GOODNESS

Sometimes, if we're halfway lucky,
we may stumble & glimpse goodness
in a face, peering around a corner
or sharp turn in the labyrinth.
We arrive, staring over our shoulder
at pawprints the snow leopard left
on a trail circling back to the most fierce
hunter, back to the uncoiled loop's
double roundel. On how many paths
do we dare seek the spun knot
beneath the plum tree bent down
with blooms in the Middle Kingdom?
We brainstormed over bowls of water
spinach, Chinese broccoli, crispy fish,
& Szechuan beef. I can still see
stations of the cross we walked
through the Village, as if taunted
by springtime. Weren't we in Shangri-la
for happy hour? With so much laughter
in your eyes & mouth, I didn't know you
could foresee crocuses in the snow
as those perfect nocturnal beings
wrestled day & night to the ground.
George, I'd love to believe nature
is never truly unkind, that she

only wills the tiger bee its stinger
to guard the rally of honeysuckle
climbing the rusty iron-spiked gate
where mercy pulled all the fruit
down to the lowest branches.

A VOICE ON AN
ANSWERING MACHINE

I can't erase her voice. If I opened the door to the cage & tossed the magpie into the air, a part of me would fly away, leaving only the memory of a plucked string trembling in the night. The voice unwinds breath, soldered wires, chance, loss, & digitalized impulse. She's telling me how light pushed darkness till her father stood at the bedroom door dressed in a white tunic. Sometimes we all wish we could put words back into our mouths.

I have a plant of hers that has died many times, only to be revived with less water & more light, always reminding me of the voice caught inside the little black machine. She lives between the Vale of Kashmir & nirvana, beneath a bipolar sky. The voice speaks of an atlas & a mask, a map of Punjab, an ugly scar from college days on her abdomen, the unsaid credo, but I still can't make the voice say, Look, I'm sorry. I've been dead for a long time.

THE BEAUTIFUL QUICKNESS OF A STREET BOY

Where did he come from, this boy
pressing his face against the window
of the car on that January afternoon
in Burdwan? One of the three coins
slips from my outstretched fingers
& falls somewhere in the small car,
& I contort my body to retrieve
this touch of alloyed copper.
Then I look up at the boy
pointing to the roses on the dashboard.
Afternoon light falls between us.
I hand him a rose, & he walks away
with his nose pushed into the bloom,
smiling to himself. In no time
the boy is facing a young man
waiting on the platform.
They exchange a few words.
The man shoves a hand into his pocket
& gives the boy a coin,
& he dances away, leaving the man
holding the flower behind his back.

Our car fills with awe & laughter,
& someone says, There's a woman
somewhere. That street boy,
as if he'd sprung out of me,
out of another time,
is still pleading with everything
he knows—his dusty clothes
& eyes lit by Shiva,
his smile & black hair
alive with lice, & his wounded song—
as a bearded monkey paces
the train station's roof spine.

LAST OF THE MONKEY GODS

They moon temple ghosts, swinging on heavy doors.
They ride rabid dogs in the alleys of ill repute.
They decipher the language of crows at dawn
in ancient trees, the blueness of a god's skin.
They tiptoe power lines, rope bridges around the city.
They throw stones at the ambassador's sedan.
When afternoon prayers begin, they grow silent,
lying in each other's arms, dreaming of clemency.

The monkeys are now rounding up street boys.
At least, at first, it seems this is true, but in no time
the boys learn to single out a monkey in the throng
& wrestle him to the ground. He may try to bite
& scratch, to howl & cry ceremoniously, to plead
with the one word he knows, but then the fight
goes out of him when the rest of his great clan
returns to jabbering & the sacred picking of lice.

The boys zap him with a small laser gun.
A garnet of mute bells is tossed into the dust,
& chants go aeons back to the beginning & die.

The fearless illumination goes out of his eyes.
The boys tag him. He rises to wander freely.
As naked unholiness crawls into the night,
they're wrestled one by one to the ground
& castrated for the music of coins jangling in a pocket.

GONE

Somebody is screaming. I spring to my feet,
half stumbling out of the brain's cloudy weather.
Where am I, what year of the Rat, Horse, Dragon,
or Snake is it? I'm out the door. In the hallway.
Damn. I'm pulling on my See No Evil T-shirt.
A woman's no-no voice. Bach usually drifts
out into this hall. This is Beethoven. I mean,
I hear doors slam & the struggle of an elevator.
The biblical howl of a gale. I hear a man's voice.
He's crying in a language between two or three
languages. The Chinese couple down the hall
on the left. I said hello, & they looked at the floor.
When I said goodbye, they gazed through me.
I hear running feet across the floorboards.
I raise a hand to knock. What year of the Monkey,
Wild Boar, or Goat is this? I retreat behind my door.
I listen. I listen with my head & heart. The body.
The cells. I can hear a sobbing inside the walls.
I don't want to listen anymore. I fall across the bed
with my clothes & shoes on. I can't. Somewhere
a saxophone plays in Shanghai. Next morning
I ask the doorman what happened last night
on my floor. He shakes his head & speaks

slowly. Where am I? What year of the Hare
or Ox is this? I walk through the city, hurting
for a clue, but I can't find laughter because
I was listening to the wind when their baby
swallowed a little lead bird from China
& flew away from here.

TOGETHERNESS

Someone says Tristan
& Isolde, the shared cup
& broken vows binding them,
& someone else says Romeo
& Juliet, a lyre & Jew's harp
sighing a forbidden oath,
but I say a midnight horn
& a voice with a moody angel
inside, the two married rib
to rib. Of course, I am
thinking of those Tuesdays
or Thursdays at Billy Berg's
in L.A. when Lana Turner would say,
Please sing "Strange Fruit"
for me, & then her dancing
nightlong with Mel Tormé,
as if she knew what it took
to make brass & flesh say yes
beneath the clandestine stars
& a spinning that is so fast
we can't feel the planet moving.
Is this why some of us fall
in & out of love? Did Lady Day

& Prez ever hold each other
& plead to those notorious gods?
I don't know. But I do know
even if a horn & voice plumb
the unknown, what remains unsaid
coalesces around an old blues
& begs with a hawk's yellow eyes.

ADONIS IN THE BIG APPLE

He leans a silhouette against the shop-
window, questioning his reflection.
Yes, tonight he looks slightly older
in the murderous light. Once, years ago,
when women & men danced around him,
smiling, when he was called Adonis
of the art world, his six-four frame
made him feel absolutely Apollo
as the rich & powerful gazed up.

He had learned to use their fetishes
against them. His abridged footnotes
to the history of those broken hearts
are forgiven. A bouquet of rare wine
is on his breath, & he says to the plate glass:
I'd play "Jack the Bear" day & night,
but placed Bach on the turntable
when Cinderella came for the slipper
she left under my bed on Avenue A.

He knew the secrets of folk medicine
& outsider art, but Renoir, Rossetti,
& Edward Hopper owned his tongue

at those uptown parties & soirees.
He had touched Solomon's seal,
but what did he know about chancery
& mysteries of the dead? He knows
there's no loneliness like springtime
alone in this city, no journey as mad

as pursuing a lovely ghost in a crowd.
When lovers leaned against his chest,
the scent of fish seeped from his village
into their dreams. He says, Why can't
a weakness be my salvation? Tonight
the one wearing a lime green silk dress
& pearls, how did her stare wound me?
Once I would have just closed my eyes
& let the smell of the sea carry me home.

THE WINDOW DRESSER'S SONG

We tango till light slants obscenely
down to naked souls. Step for step,
note for note, they follow me up
from the basement & across the floor,
& then I glide each into a big glass box
where everything begs the passing eye.
We waltz every phrase the body darcs
to translate, stolen from a milonga
on a corner back in Buenos Aires,
saying, Now your trousseau's silk . . .
They come from the outer boroughs
with endangered songs in their heads.
My great flair for hues & stripes
wows them on this city sidewalk,
poses my mannequins perfect
behind Plexiglas. We slow dance
till our window is a split personality
of translucency, a ripple of chiffon,
& the lightest cotton from India.
We say how to move, how to be.
Lord, the curves I lean into are
reckless as any other revelation.
If colors & styles clash, a hip
or head swivel, the lift of a hand
or tilt of a lamp can fix twilight.

DEAR MR. DECOY

If it weren't for you, I wouldn't be
    smooth as morning light on cold stone.
I walk into a jewelry store ten paces behind you
    & look them in the eye like a pawnbroker
when I wear this apple red lipstick
    & blush of Icelandic rouge.
I lean lightly on the showcase in a low-cut
    flair of tailored innocence. You could be
the lost descendant of some South African
    whose fingernails were checked at dusk
for a speck of gold. Your face
    blurs their brainy maps, & I apologize
for using their image of you this way,
    as if we agreed to rendezvous
among twelve misty stations of the cross.
    I run my hands through blond hair
till I own the store, my slender fingers
    toying with silver latches & the glint
of diamonds. I know you are a good man
    who worked & squirreled away coins
for small dreams, unable to stop seeing her
    wearing this necklace, a secret wad
of dollars pressed against your bad
    heart. Their cameras never aim at me,

Mr. Decoy. I play with a sapphire brooch
        as if I'm one of Pindar's Graces
or Charites, but I live for the fit & tug
        of blue jeans as my hips sway to "Uh
La La La." I never clutch my foolish purse
        when you pass. Texas pours out
my mouth, & I know how to reach so my skirt
        rides up my thighs. The mink collar
of my cashmere sweater blinks its jade
        eyes. Years ago Jennifer dared me, & now
it's habit woven into flesh, Mr. Decoy,
        & sometimes I can't stop myself
from clowning with the light this way.

EDDIE, THE IMMUNE

I was a fine altar boy, yes.
They say I was also angelic,
whatever it means this side of hell.
My heroes have blood on their hands,
& they all look exactly like me.
A good suit. A tilt of the hat.
A perfect, practiced smile.
A white handkerchief in my breast pocket.
Shoes polished till I can see
miracles in the corners of everyday
lives. See her? I was born to read
her mind. I can get so close to her
my breath is cool on her skin,
& she'll be seven blocks away
when a cry leaps into her throat
& she knows I untied the money belt
hidden under her velvet jacket.
On the el headed south of the lake,
I get so close to this gentleman
he believes I am his lost brother. "Trust"
is the code word in my gentle profession.
My pigeon hands over his life to me
for a second. I was the perfect altar boy.

Bless this bread. This wine. This body.
This blood. You see, the color of eyes
makes my job so easy in the Midwest.
I think, Someday I'll give up this racket,
hightail it out to gorgeous Hollywood,
& let some hotshot talk me into the movies.
I'm Eddie, but on this side of town
everybody calls me mister.

THE THORN MERCHANT'S GODSON

Tonight Raymond comes as Apollonius of Tyana.
Pretty as a girl, he's unpredictable.
He's journeyed to eastern Europe
for this spinout bachelor party,
lugging a ball 'n' chain from bar
to bar, in lockstep with his buddies
from Dallas. Actually, Raymond
is dangerous. He was a starling at twilight,
but with these guys talons sprout
as he gooses barmaids & swills down vodka.
He'd do any unkind thing for a joke.
But favors buy favors in the underworld.
The gift his godfather gave him sways on a shiny chain.
He or she, George or Georgianna, he is still Raymond.
Cold-cocked by too much joy for one man,
there's something about tugging an iron ball
seems almost natural for him, as if a phantom
prejudged the heaviness before he lifted it.
What dark favor is owed whom?
The name of this club—The Rose of Iopolis—
whispered into an ear two thousand miles
away. Why crack a man's skull
to defend his father's good name?

Raymond rubs his eyes & wonders
why the television's so damn loud.
Where is he? There's a perfume
that goes back to the island of Kos,
to the pillar. How did he get here?
The naked blonde on the bed,
is she alive or dead? The gift
is the weight of a pocket watch
ticking like a fat slug of gold
pressed against his groin.

ONTOLOGY & GUINNESS

Darling, my daddy's razor strop
is in my hands, & there's a soapy cloud
on my face. I'm a man of my word.
Didn't I say, If Obama's elected,
I'll shave off this damn beard
that goes back to '68, to Chicago?
I know, I also said I'd kiss the devil,
but first let me revise this contract.
I can taste tear gas. I hear a blur
of billy clubs when I hit the drums.
I haven't witnessed this mug shot
in decades, but I'm facing the mirror.
I'm still the same man. Almost.
Led Zeppelin is still in my nogginbox.
Alan Watts, old guru of ghosts
& folksingers, I can still two-step
& do-si-do to Clifton Chenier.
But, in no time, this philosopher
will be going down the drain, baby.
Look at how a finely honed razor works.
I may be a taxi driver, but I know time
opens an apple seed to find a worm.
See, I told you, my word is gold,

good as making a wager against
the eternal hush. The older I get
the quicker Christmas comes,
but if I had to give up the heavenly
taste of Guinness dark, I couldn't
live another goddamn day. Darling,
you can chisel that into my headstone.

Notes

"Kindness" is for Carol Rigolot.

"English" is dedicated to the memory of Andrzei Ciecwierz.

"Flesh" is for Antonella Francini.

"Ode to the Guitar" is for Flavio Cucchi.

"Goodness" is dedicated to the memory of George Lin.